SPORTS ENCYCLOPEDIA

BALL SPORTS II AND COMBAT SPORTS

Om KIDZ
An imprint of Om Books International

Contents

Throwball

Throwball is a very popular game played exclusively by women. This game is popular in Asia. It is considered to be an equivalent of volleyball for women.

Origin

Like volleyball, the origin of throwball is also rooted in the YMCA. It originated in the1930s in England and Australia, and eventually came to India when Chennai held the first tournament for women in the 1940s.

When the game reached Bengaluru in the1950s, a nationwide tournament was held. The Throwball Federation of India was formed in 1978, which conducts the biggest throwball tournament in India. Initially started as a "women only" sport, it has now become a unisex sport.

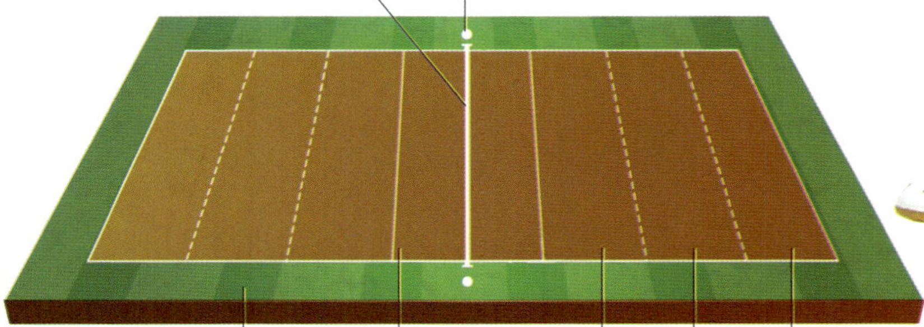

Fact card

- This sport was originally played only by women in India.
- Throwball was started for women, but eventually men started playing the game too.
- The National Throwball Championship is annually held in India.

Equipment required to play

Poles

The poles should be between 8 cm and 10 cm, and the height has to be measured from the playing surface. The poles should be made of metal and painted in white.

Each pole should be fixed exactly in the centre of the court with a distance of 0.50 m.

There should be a metal pulley on top of the pole to tie the net.

Net

The net should be made up of either cotton or nylon, which should be 12.2 m long and 1 m wide.

Size of the mesh (square) shall be 10 cm × 10 cm.

The ribbon should be 5 cm thick at the top and the bottom of the net. The cord runs through it to support the net.

Net height from the centre should be 2.30 m.

The Ball

The size of the ball when inflated, should be between 70 and 72 cm in circumference. It should weigh between 400 and 450 g. Only balls marked with the official TFI logo are allowed in tournaments.

Antenna

The antenna should be fixed on either side of the net. It should be 1.80 m long with a diameter of 10 mm, made of cane or fibre. It should be projected 80 cm above the net.

Golf

"Fore!" yells the golfer. Before taking a shot, he must warn others on the golf-course about his plan to hit a hard projectile at a very high speed. Despite such dangers, golf is considered to be a gentleman's game.

Origin

Some historians trace the golf's origin back to the Roman game of paganica. In paganica, participants used a bent stick to hit a stuffed leather ball. One theory states that paganica spread throughout Europe as the Romans conquered most of the continent during the first century BCE. From there, it eventually evolved into the modern game that we know today.

Contemporary beliefs suggest that the early forms of golf were first played in the Netherlands and then in Scotland.

Golf came into being only a little before the fifteenth century. The game might be conceived as a domesticated form of medieval games, such as football. As a result, strength, speed and violence were replaced by judgement and skill.

Golf has been documented as being played at the St Andrews Links in Fife, Scotland in United Kingdom as early as 1552. It is certified as the world's oldest golf course by the Guinness World Records.

The Masters, the US Open, the Open Championship (or the British Open) and the PGA Championship are the four most prestigious men's tournaments of golf. These are considered to be the sport's major championships.

Rules

The rules of golf are complex and are maintained by the R&A (a spin-off of the Royal and Ancient Golf club of St Andrews).

The ball has to be teed within a club length of the previous hole.

The tee is kept on the ground. The ball struck from the tee is not to be changed. A player can take his/her ball out of water to play.

Golf is played on a number of courses, with varying number of holes. The most popular number selected for the holes is 18.

A golfer putting the golf ball in one of the holes on the ground using a putter club which is used to make short distance shots.

For each hole target to be played, the starting point has to be the teeing ground. Two markers mark out the front. The teeing ground is the two clubs long rectangular space, which is directly behind the marker lines. The player tees his/her ball anywhere within that space.

Teeing is the process of setting up the ball on a small wooden or plastic peg (called a tee), from where he/she strikes it toward the hole.

There are two distinct forms of play; match play and stroke or medal play. In match play, the player and his/her opponent are playing together and competing only against each other.

Stroke play is used in tournaments in which, each competitor is competing against every other player in the tournament. Match play treats each hole as a round and the one who gets it in fewer strokes wins the round. In stroke play, the competitor who successfully scores the stipulated rounds in the fewest strokes is considered to be the winner.

A driver club is used to hit the golf ball when covering long distances.

A wedge club is used to get the ball on the greens from hazardous areas like sand pits.

A set of golf clubs is carried in a bag made of fibre so that it is light to carry.

Wall of fame

American golfer Eldrick Tont "Tiger" Woods is the most successful golfers of all time. He has been one of the highest-paid athletes in the world.

The winner of 18 major championships during his career, American golfer Jack Nicklaus is known as the "golden bear".

Professional golfer Sandra Post was the first Canadian to play the LPGA tour.

Fact card

- Golf requires extensive equipment and is an expensive sport to play. In many places, playing golf is a symbol of status.
- China banned the development of golf courses some years ago. Despite this, the number of courses has tripled.
- The longest recorded drive was about 470 m by Michael Hoke Austin.

Tchoukball

Tchoukball is an indoor ball sport. In this unique sport, the players have to move quickly, perform many jumps and be very athletic.

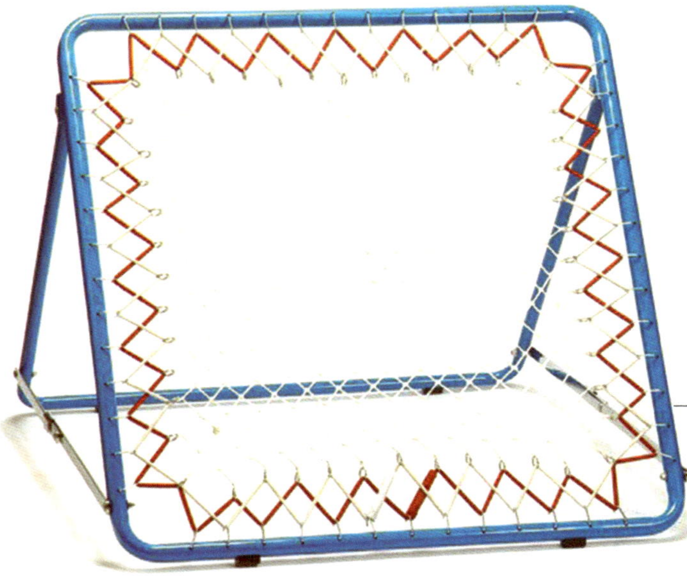

This is a frame. To score a point, the ball must bounce off of this frame and go past the 'D' without being caught by a defending player.

Origin

Tchoukball was developed by a Swiss biologist named Hermann Brandt. It was invented back in 1970. He created this game as a safer alternative to other ball sports which caused the players several injuries. He wanted the game to be less aggressive with less contact.

He wanted to create a game where teamwork and safety came first. He wanted to create a more humane and tolerant society through this sport. Tchoukball is a mix of handball, volleyball and squash.

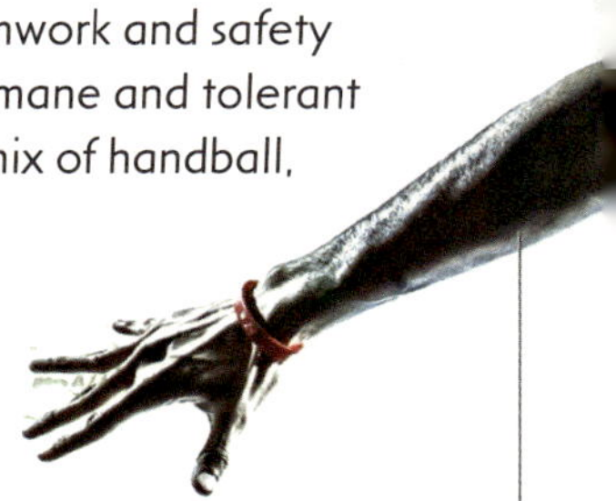

A player cannot hold the ball for longer than three seconds. He cannot bounce the ball.

Court of Tchoukball

- The court is generally a 20 m × 40 m rectangle. There is one rebound frame at each end.
- There is a D-shaped semicircle area measuring 3 m in radius. It is the "forbidden zone".
- The lines marking a zone are a part of that zone. The D-shaped semicircle marking the forbidden zone is a part of the forbidden zone.

Rules

Each team has seven players. The objective of the game is to score by throwing the ball at the frame on the opponent's side in such a way that it bounces outside the D-shaped forbidden zone measuring 3 m in radius. The ball should not be caught by a member of the opponent's team.

This is a non-contact sport so physical contact between players is strictly forbidden. A defending team cannot intercept an attacking team's pass.

The players must take three steps while holding the ball. They must only hold it for three seconds and cannot pass the ball more than three times before trying to score.

An attacking team player tries to score while the defending team players get ready to catch the ball once it bounces.

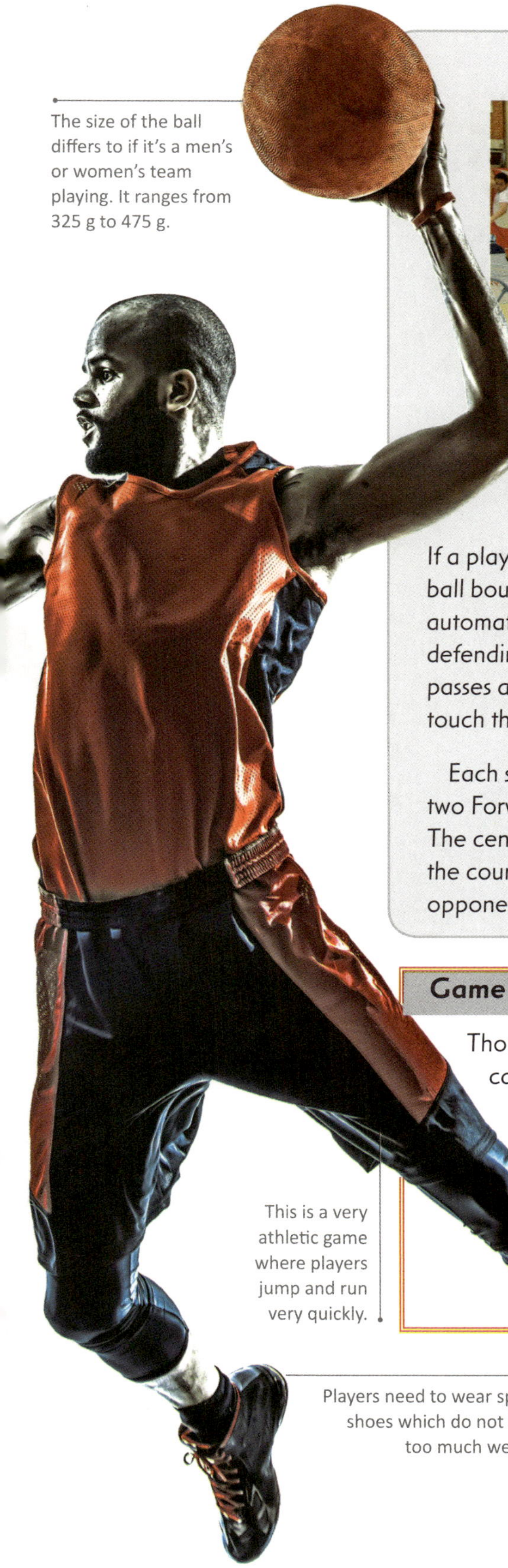

The size of the ball differs to if it's a men's or women's team playing. It ranges from 325 g to 475 g.

This is a very athletic game where players jump and run very quickly.

Players need to wear sports shoes which do not have too much weight.

As it is a non-contact sport, members cannot interfere with the player trying to make a pass or score.

If a player drops a pass, which means that the ball bounces on the court, the possession is automatically passed to the other team. The defending team is not allowed to interfere with passes and attempts to score. The players cannot touch the ball with their legs, feet, chest or knees.

Each side has two Right Wings, two Left Wings, two Forward Pivots and one Centre Pivot player. The centre pivot is positioned at the centre of the court, while the other players travel with the opponent player.

Game equipment

Though there are two frames, either team can score at either frame. The frame is similar to a trampoline rather than a net, as the ball bounces off of the frame with some force. This is similar to squash. The ball is similar to the one used in the sport of handball.

The International Tchoukball or the Federation Internationale de Tchoukball (FITB) regulates the rules of the sport. There are World Tchoukball Championships held annually. There are 13 member associations and 22 affiliated associations with the FITB.

The World Tchoukball Championship is held for male and female teams. The Republic of China has been the most successful in all categories. There are also M-18 male and M-18 female categories held, but these championships were started in 2005.

Wall of fame

Elvis Tan is the captain of the Republic Polytechnic Men's team. He participates in the Inter-Tertiary Championship with his team. The RP team won the 2013-14 tournament.

Nico QUEK Ping Yang played in the South East Asia Tchoukball Championship as the vice-captain of his team. Their coach was ANG Kian Hwee.

The Republic of China's tchoukball team wears red and white colours. They are the most successful team.

Fact card

- The first World Tchoukball Championships were held in the Republic of China in 1984. The home team won the All Men and All Women categories.
- The first M-18 Championships were held in the Republic of China in 1984. It was won by Switzerland.
- India hosted the Asia-Pacific Tchoukball Championships in 2003. The Republic of China won the All Men and All Women categories.

Dodgeball

In this sport, the players try to hit each other with a ball in order to score. It is a highly competitive and fast-paced game. It is popular in North America.

The dodgeball is heavier than a netball. It is the same size as a volleyball.

Origin

Dodgeball originated in Africa more than 200 years ago. Its aim was to build team spirit. If one was injured, the rest of the team members protected him/her by eliminating the opponents. The earliest version of the game used rocks instead of rubber balls.

Later on, the methods of playing the game were changed. The rock was changed to a leather ball and the field's size was increased. Presently, the game is mostly played in elementary schools and high schools. It is a very popular game in North America and Europe.

A player is aiming at an opponent team player.

Rules

The major objective of the game is to eliminate the opposition team members by marking them with the ball. This game has very strict rules so that it remains fair and safe.

The game starts by a "rush off" when the ball is kept on the central line and both the teams have to rush in order to grab possession of the ball. If a person is hit with the ball "on the full", i.e., without any rebound from anywhere, the person is said to be "out". The only way through which the ball is considered to be "dead" is when one member of the opponent team holds it in their hand.

A player must try and catch the ball thrown from the opponent's team. The player must try to hold the ball for more than two seconds. If this happens, the thrower gets eliminated.

If a ball is declared dead, the teams again try to gain possession. The player that gets possession must hit the opponent team player with the ball. If the player picks up the ball from the opponents' zone, then the player is considered out.

The game is over once all the players of a team get eliminated. The players cannot kick the ball. If a player is caught throwing the ball at another player's head, or above the groin area, they are out. "Opening rush" is the fastest part of the game when players try to get possession.

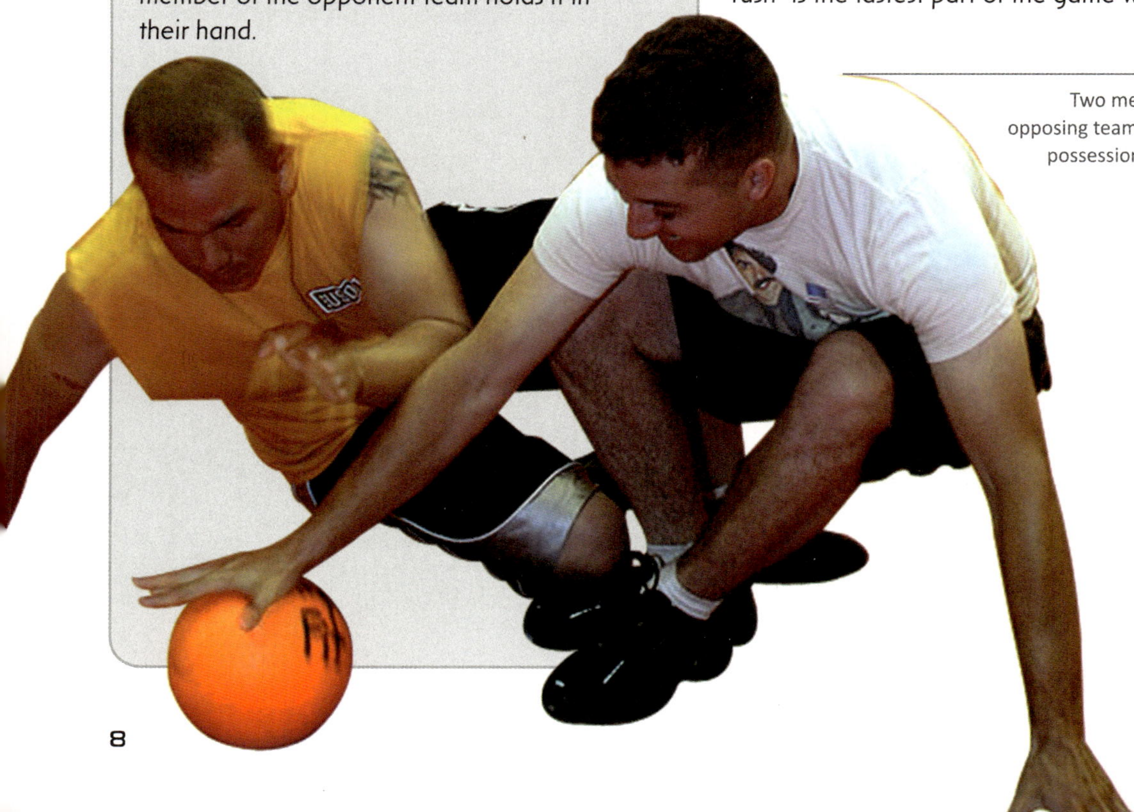

Two members from opposing teams try to gain possession of the ball.

Fact card

- Dodgeball teams usually use 3 to 10 dodgeballs. Each ball is of a similar size to that of a volleyball.
- During one match, 6048 players played the game. This is a world record in the dodgeball game.
- "Sekan-tadi" is an Indian variation of the dodgeball game.

Angleball

Angleball is an indoor field sport combining the skills utilised in basketball and football.

Origin

Invented in the 1960s, the game of angleball started as a pre-exercise session for both football and basketball sports. Soon it was realised that the pre-exercise session had the potential of becoming a separate game all on its own. That's how angleball was born. Inter-college competitions started taking place which gained immense popularity. Currently it has been adopted as a pre-season training session by the NFL.

A group of children playing the game of angleball in an indoor field.

Rules

Angleball is a light-contact sport which requires accuracy, skill, agility and speed. Two large balls are kept on top of the two poles, placed at opposite sides of the field. Being a mixture of football and basketball, the teams keep passing a smaller ball back and forth, in order to drop the opponent team's ball off that perch.

One goal marks one point. Any player from the offense time, if touched by the defensive player, has only three seconds to stop and pass the ball. If not, the possession of the ball changes and the tagged player cannot score a goal for that period.

If the big ball is knocked off from the perch on the opposite side, then it's a goal. The smaller balls can both be thrown and kicked by the players. There is no goalkeeper in this game, but there is a restricted area where a player from the offensive team is not allowed to enter.

The size of the pitch is decided as per the game's requirement. It is usually kept between 30–35 yards. The highest scoring team in the game becomes the winning team.

Players can only make contact with the player who has possession of the ball.

The players cannot make contact with each other for any other purpose.

In this picture, a player has managed to knock off the opponent's ball.

Fact card

- The name "angleball" is derived from the name of the creator "Engle".

Tetherball

This is a two-player game. It gets its name from the use of a ball which is tethered to a pole. It is a very popular North American game.

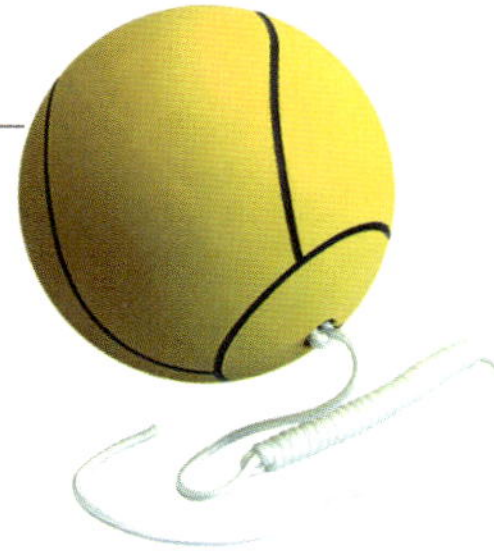

The ball comes attached with a rope which is tethered to a pole.

Origin

This is a North American sport which was first described in Jessie H. Bancroft's book called "Games for the Playground" in 1909. At the time, a tethered tennis ball was used, which was hit with racquets.

Rules

The objective of this game is to win by making the ball roll around the pole. One player sends it around and the other player tries to change its direction. If the other player does not manage to do this, the first player wins. This is a very simple game to play and involves two people. The game begins when the first person yells, "side and ways".

The player is allowed to hit the ball with an open palm or a fist and swing it around the pole in whichever direction he/she wishes to. Once the ball is hit, the opponent's task is to alter that direction. The first player cannot touch the ball until the opponent touches it back. The ball is tied by a tether to a stationary pole. The game ends when the ball gets completely wrapped around the pole and hits it.

The ball is slightly larger than a tennis ball.

The pole can be wooden or metal.

The opponent player needs to be patient and wait for the ball to come to his side.

In another version of the game, players use racquets instead of their hands and stand away from each other. They try to send the ball back and forth until one person misses.

Fact card

- Tetherball originated from a game that was very violent and was played among army officers to induce fear into the opponents' minds.

There is a line on the pole that shows where the ball should reach in order to declare a player as the winner. A certain match can go on for two or more sets to decide the fate of the game. Originally, a volleyball was used and it was tethered to the pole.

If a player commits a foul by not following the mentioned rules, there is a change in possession and the game is restarted.

It is a two-player game. But in camps, the teachers or instructors make pairs among the players and have them take turns. The game can go on until someone is declared a winner. Usually, each pair gets one chance to play.

The players must strictly stand on their side of the pole. If a player moves to the other side, it is counted as a foul. If the player catches the ball and then throws it, it is a foul. The player needs to hit the ball. Catching or holding the ball is not allowed.

If the player touches the rope instead of the ball, it is a foul. If the player hits the ball twice, it is counted as a foul.

Fistball

Fistball is a game which was invented in Europe. It is very similar to volleyball because the players try to pass the ball over a net. However, they hit the ball with their closed fists.

Origin

While the details of the invention of this game is not very clear, what is known is that the game originated in Europe. Most people believe that the game was started in Italy as the Roman Emperor Gordian III mentioned the game first in the year 240. In 1555, Antonius Scaiono listed the rules of the game.

Fistball came to Germany in 1870. It was introduced by Georg Weber. Today, Germany is the world champion of fistball. However, at the time that it was introduced, the rules of scoring and playing were quite different from what they are today. Germany saw a drop in the game during World War I. It later picked up again in 1927.

A player's foot cannot touch the service line.

Rules

Fistball is played between two teams. Each team has five players. Like the game of volleyball, the fistball court is divided into two halves. These halves are marked by a centre line. The net stands here. The net is spread between two posts which are at a height of 2 m.

Players can send the ball to the opponent's side using their closed fist or their arm. If the opponent's fail to return the shot, then the team scores a point.

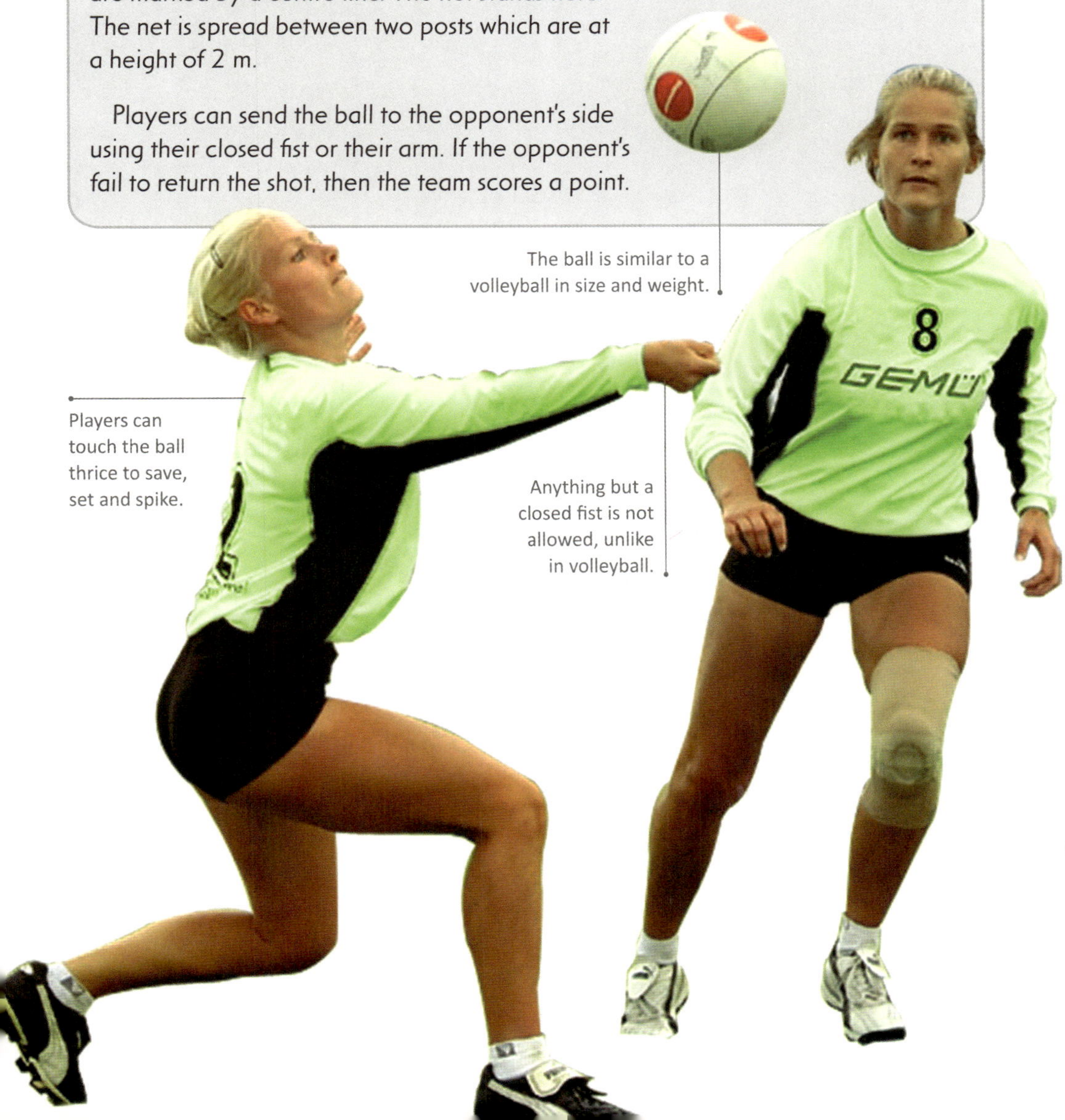

The ball is similar to a volleyball in size and weight.

Players can touch the ball thrice to save, set and spike.

Anything but a closed fist is not allowed, unlike in volleyball.

The team cannot make contact with the ball more than three times. The ball can bounce once on the team's half of the court. However, no member of the team can hit the ball twice.

If the ball touches the net, or if a player touches the net or a post, then it is considered a foul. The ball cannot touch the portion outside the marked field. If the ball touches the ground twice in succession, then it is a foul. The ball can only touch a player's fist or arm. If it touches any other part, then the team loses a point. If a player uses the foot to touch the ball, it is a foul. If the player's foot is put past the service line or end line, it is a foul and the score is not counted.

Fact card

- The International Fistball Association (IFA) was formed in 1960.

Bowling

Bowling is one of the most famous indoor ball games. In this game, a ball is thrown along a lane to knock down the pins arranged at the end of that lane. Bowling is a popular sport in many countries.

Origin

Bowling is said to have been invented in Ancient Egypt. Evidences of this game have been found in Ancient Rome as well. The excavations conducted in Ancient Egypt produced large balls used for bowling back in 3200 BCE. These balls were made with husks of grain, covered with leather and stitched together with strings.

Bowling was also played in 400 CE Germany, but as a religious ritual to cleanse the soul of sin, by rolling a rock into a kegel. The ones who used to perform these rituals were called "keglers".

It came to England in 1299. Here, the more or less modern form of bowling came to be practiced. King Edward III banned the game in 1336 as it was distracting people from the practice of archery. Bowling lanes came to be in London in 1455. As they were made indoors, bowling became an all-weather game. Bowling is called "kegelbahns" in Germany.

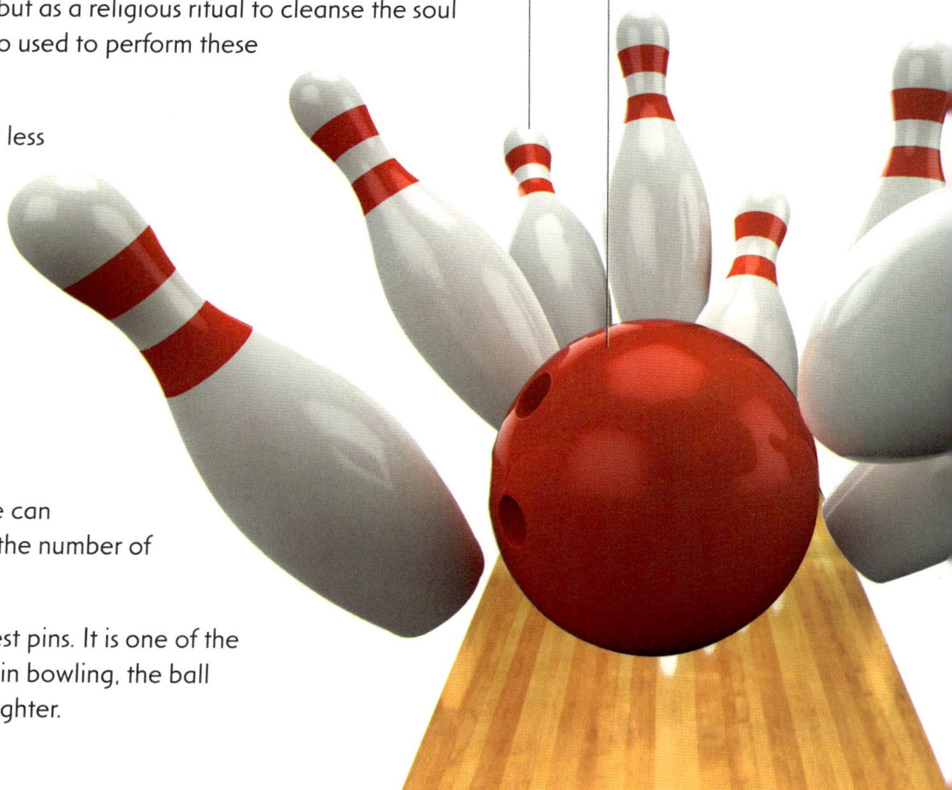

If all the pins at the end of the lane fall, then it is called a "strike". It is a perfect shot.

The bowling ball has three holes to put the thumb and the two middle fingers.

Gameplay

There are numerous variations of bowling. People can differentiate between the variations by counting the number of pins stacked at the end of the lane.

10-pin bowling has a larger ball and the heaviest pins. It is one of the most widely played versions of bowling. In nine-pin bowling, the ball does not have finger holes and the pins are also lighter.

However, the general rules for all of variations are the same. There is a bowling line which a player is not supposed to cross. The player is allowed to run and throw the ball staying within that line only.

Crossing the line is considered a foul. It can lead to the disqualification of the player. On top of that, crossing the line can also be dangerous because the lane ahead the line is made oily for the ball to glide on it.

Thus, crossing the line can cause the person to slip on the lane, resulting in injuries. A person cannot use more than one bowling lane at any given time. The score is checked on one lane only.

In this photo, you can see the line behind which the bowler is standing. It is from here that he sends the ball forward.

Bowling balls automatically roll into the bowling ball range. The players select the bowling ball from here. The lane is where the balls glide to reach the pin area.

The pins are arranged in a Fibonacci triangle. They are all of the same size and weight. They are also of the same colour. All pins are equal. The score is given according to how many pins fall after the ball hits it. The lowest score goes to the player if he or she does not manage to hit any pin. After three times, the player loses their place in the line up. If the player hits three strikes in a row, they get extra points on the score screen.

This is the bowling rack. Balls are arranged for the player to choose the one best suitable to them.

If a player knocks out all the pins in one go, it is called a "strike". If he/she knocks out all the pins in the second chance, it is called as a "spare".

Usually the balls are classified according to their weight so that the player can decide which ball to select for the remaining amount of pins in the lane.

There are different bowling shoes that are available. Normal tennis shoes are not allowed on the alley. There are some special shoes with a slider sole and a breaking sole. The shoes have to be chosen in such a way that they provide the best grip on the lane surface. The scoring is done based on the number of pins claimed in number of attempts.

Special flat shoes are worn for bowling. They grip the ground better.

Bowling can be played as a team sport or even an individual sport. There is no disadvantage to age, gender or skill.

Certain players tend to grip the bowling ball differently. However, it is important to ensure that the grip is proper so the fingers don't get injured.

Wall of fame

Norm Duke is a five-time world champion bowler who bowled 64 perfect 300 games.

Peter Weber is a four-time world champion in 10-pin bowling.

Walter Ray Williams Jr has total earnings of over USD 4.5 million during this career.

Earl Anthony won six "Bowler of the Year" awards and 43 championship bowling games.

Fact card

- There is no such thing as a "minimum weight" for the bowling balls.
- A bowling ball can have a maximum of 12 finger holes.
- Some charity events hold bowling contests and amateur bowling nights to raise money. The sport of bowling raises over USD 225 million a year for charity.

Wallyball

Wallyball is sometimes referred to as "rebound volleyball" because the games are so similar in fashion.

Origin

Wallyball was founded in 1979 at a sports club in California. It was created in 1979. It started off as a modification of volleyball. The inventers of the game wanted to attract more customers to the sports club during the summer break. Volleyball was a popular sport then so the modified game was hyped to be even better. But eventually it got picked up as a competitive sport and earned its own fan base. Wallyball is a combination of tennis, volleyball and handball.

This player is jumping high in order to spike the ball and send it to the other team.

Regular sports shoes are used by the wallyball players.

Wallyball also uses the save and spike technique.

Rules

Wallyball can be played in two teams, each of the teams having two to four players. This number is fixed in a professional championship contest. It is usually played in a racquetball court. There are two service areas on each side. The ball used is spherical in shape and is markedly different than a volleyball in appearance.

Like volleyball, this game uses the system of rally scoring or speed scoring. There is a freeze point, which is decided before the game begins. Teams must score three points before the match point.

A player must serve the ball to the other team. Then the rallying system begins.

Legal spin is done by contacting the ball off-centre as it is struck.

Every service earns the teams a point. This stops only when the freeze point arrives. If this happens, then a point is given to the next side-out. After this, each team must serve to score points. The freeze point arrives at different times, depending on how many points are needed to win the game. The "match point" is the total score needed to win the game. The "freeze point" is three points below that.

In a three-person team, players use a blocker to block the ball, a defender and the front-line defender who throws shots outside the bounds of the field.

Fact card

- The Wallyball Information Network (WIN) regulates the game.

COMBAT SPORTS

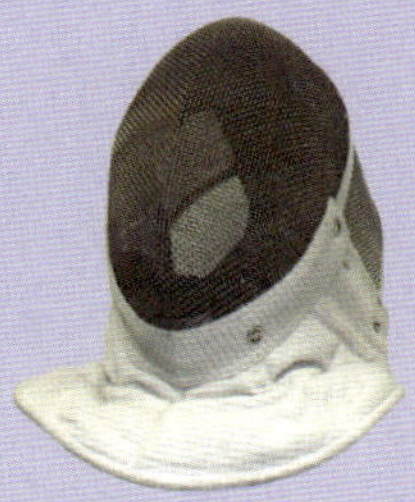

The one term that adequately describes combat sports and all the people who partake in it is, "fighting spirit"! It shows enthusiasm and zeal. This is the core of many sports originated from the art of combat. In combat sports or fighting sports, two players fight with each other in a one-on-one setup.

Depending upon the nature, combat sports can either be partially or fully based on contact with the opponent. Based on the techniques used in them, combat sports are widely divided into grappling, striking and weapons sports. However, there are some modern combat sports like MMA and Muay Thai which use both grappling and striking techniques.

A match can either have a fixed time frame or it might go on until the opponent is defeated. Winning the match also depends on either scoring the maximum points within the stipulated time or defeating the opponent. In the latter instance, the winning is considered to be more of an outright victory.

Let's take a look at the different combat sports. Three, two, one and fight!

Did you know? In order to reduce the risk of brain damage resulting from fighting injuries, fighters are advised to take fish oil supplements. It provides the necessary DHA for recovering from brain damage.

Fencing

"En garde!" Swashbuckling swordplay has long been a coveted skill. Today, there are world championship fencing competitions. It is one of the five performances featured in the modern Olympic Games.

Origin

The first mention of formal fencing or sword fighting was made nearly 3000 years ago in Egypt. Since then, every culture had some type of reference in books about sword fighting. Contesting against opponents with a sword later became less of a fight and more of a method to showcase and improve skills. The Gladiators of Ancient Rome are an example of this.

"Gladiators" fought with small swords called "gladius". After the fall of the Roman Empire, the duelling tradition continued into the middle ages and transformed into an elegant sport. However, after the invention of guns and gunpowder, the use of swords or close-contact fighting reduced on the battlefield. Swords became side arms, to be used only for ceremonial purposes. Nonetheless, they remained as a display of skill and athleticism.

Fencing is a form of swordsmanship. The art of fencing became a form of recreation for wealthy individuals. Due to the amount of funds needed to pursue this art, fencing became the symbol of acquiring "status". The knightly class, with its code of chivalry, emerged out of this.

Fencers wear a plastron, which is an underarm protector. It goes underneath the jacket and gives double protection to the fencer from the blade of the opponent. It is tied around the sword arm side and the upper arm.

Gameplay

Fencing as a modern sport was largely popularised by Domenico Angelo. It is broadly divided into three classes, based on the type of sword used.

Foil: The foil is a light, thrusting weapon. Foil fencing focuses on hitting the opponent on the neck, torso, groin and back, not anywhere else. To score, one must touch an opponent with the tip of the foil and not with the sides. One fencer must attack while the other must defend. After a point, they switch roles.

Épée: The épée is a thrusting weapon which is heavier than a foil. In épée fencing, the entire body is considered to be a valid target. Thus, the hand guard used in this type of fencing is bigger, because touching the hand would result in a point. If both the fencers touch each other at the same time, both are given points. In the case of a tie, this point is not counted and the move is considered void.

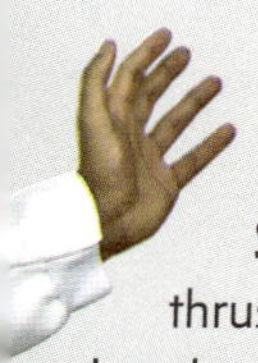

Sabre: A sabre is a light thrusting and cutting weapon. In sabre fencing, opponents hit with the sides and the tip of the blade. It is faster than the other forms of fencing. The torso is a great scoring area. However, hitting below the belt region is not allowed and can even bring negative points. The hand guard is the biggest among the three types.

Few positions during the game of fencing are:

Beat: The attacker beats the opponent's blade and continues to attack the target area.

Counter attack: It can only be played after the opponent plays an attack roll.

Step forward: To move forward one space in the game. It is used to inch closer to the opponent.

Riposte: It can only be played after a parry or beat.

Parry: This is the basic block used in the game of fencing.

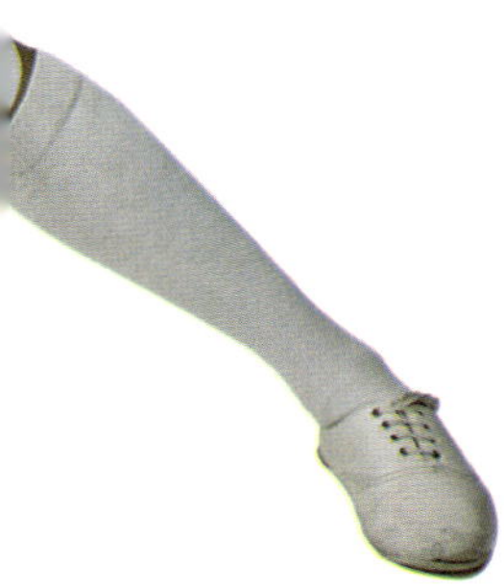

This picture is from an épée world cup final round. Both fencers can hit simultaneously.

Wall of fame

Jujie Luan is a Canadian fencer, born in China. She competed for the Chinese team in the 1984 Summer Olympics and became the first Chinese athlete to win a gold medal in fencing.

Estonian fencer from the Soviet Union, Svetlana Chirkova-Lozovaja won a gold medal for fencing at the 1968 and 1972 Summer Olympics respectively.

General George Patton of the US Army was a famous fencer. He stood fifth in fencing at the 1912 Stockholm Olympics.

Fact card

- Fencers wear white so that the hits could be easily visible. Today, other lighter colours are used.
- Modern fencers tend to wear plastic protectors to avoid confusion in the modern system of electronic scoring.
- Domenico Angelo's instructional book on fencing helped turn the sport into a recognised athletic competition around the world.

Freestyle Wrestling

Freestyle wrestling is an amateur variation of the sport. It is played all around the world. It is also contested in the Olympic Games along with the Greco-Roman wrestling style.

Freestyle wrestlers lock their limbs against an opponent's neck to take them down on the mat.

Legs must be firm on the ground in order to not lose balance.

The opponent struggles to break the lock and bring the opponent down instead.

The attacker must hold firm and use the core to bring the opponent down.

Origin

As the name implies, freestyle wrestling allows the players a wide range of techniques to defeat their opponents. Freestyle wrestling has descended from the "catch-as-catch-can" method, practised in England and the USA.

However, the Lancashire version of it has particularly influenced modern freestyle wrestling.

Freestyle wrestling became a part of the Olympic Games during the 1904 Olympics. It got its name from the Olympic competitions. The sport is regulated by the Fédération Internationale des Luttes Associées (FILA).

Wrestlers are also given a score in case they fail to pin the other down. The score decides the winner in such a case.

Rules

In freestyle wrestling, both competitors stand facing each other. Once the signal is given, they begin to inch closer. The objective is to wrestle the opponent to the ground and pin them down for a set amount of time.

If one manages to pin the opponent's shoulders down to the mat for three seconds, the former player wins outright. However, strangleholds, kicking, punching, biting or any action that may cause harm to the opponent is strictly not allowed.

Scores are awarded as follows:

- **Takedown:** The act of putting one's opponent down on the mat gains between one and five points.
- **Reversal:** The act of gaining control after being on the defensive is one point.
- **Stalling:** If the opponent flees or refuses to start, a point is awarded to the other player.

This wrestler is attempting a takedown of his opponent. The opponent must be lifted off the ground before being pinned to the floor.

Fact card

- Women's wrestling was only introduced during the Athens Olympics in 2004. Though women usually compete in seven weight classes, it is reduced to four in the Olympic competition.
- The International Olympic Committee had voted to remove the sport from the Olympics from 2020 onwards. But after great public outrage and much hue and cry, the decision had been reversed.

Greco-Roman Wrestling

Greco-Roman wrestling has been a part of the modern Olympics since the first modern Olympic Games in 1896. Several freestyle wrestling moves have been borrowed from this sport. There are different weight categories for male and female wrestlers.

Origin

The Greco-Roman wrestling style has been around since the ancient Greek and Roman civilisations. The name is given to acknowledge its presence in all civilisations formed around the Mediterranean Sea. Though many combat and body-contact sports emerged as time went on, Greco-Roman wrestling was differentiated from the rest because of the use of flat hands instead of striking hands or fists.

Over the years, this style of wrestling developed and began to look very different from the ancient Greek or Roman style of wrestling. Yet, the name remained to remind people of its long history.

The sport earned its name as a brutal combat match. Some countries considered it too violent as it had punishing moves like choke-holds, head-butting and body slams.

The Greek style of wrestling is quite different from the Greco-Roman wrestling style. But some similarities remain.

Rules

In some ways, Greco-Roman wrestling is similar to freestyle wrestling as the latter emerged from it. Players attempt to pin their opponents down to the mat to score points. However, the major difference is that the use of legs in this form is completely prohibited. Players can only use their upper body to block, pin down and fight an opponent.

As a result, one cannot make his/her opponent trip, nor can they hold them down with their legs. Also, defensive techniques like hooking one's legs behind one's opponent are forbidden.

A Greco-Roman wrestling match is played in three rounds, each lasting for two minutes. A panel of three judges scores the players.

This wrestler is attempting a body slam. The use of legs is prohibited. Only the torso and arms can be used.

All wrestlers are trained in how to get out of all the body holds used in wrestling. It is a sport of quick thinking and ability.

Fact card

- This sport takes place on a thick rubber mat to prevent injuries when players are pinned to the ground.
- Wrestlers wear singlets, a one-piece suit made of spandex. It provides comfort and flexibility. It should fit the wrestler's body tightly.

Sumo Wrestling

Sumo wrestling is a traditional Japanese form of wrestling and is still popular in Japan. The word "sumo" means to "mutually rush towards". Sumo wrestling is only practiced professionally in Japan. Though it is considered a modern martial art, it has a long history.

Origin

Sumo wrestling began as a ritual sport where a human wrestler is said to combat against a "kami", who is a divine spirit. It was conducted in the imperial courts of ancient Japan. Each province sent a wrestler to fight. This contest was called "sumai no sechie" and the word "sumo wrestling" comes from this.

Sumo wrestling became a professional sport during the Edo period for the entertainment of the public. Samurai warriors who wanted to earn an extra income, trained and fought in sumo matches. The modern sumo wrestling contests started in the Tomioka Hachiman Shrine back in 1684. Today, Osaka is the most prominent place for sumo wrestling. The Sumo Association was formed in 1925 to regulate the sport.

To this day, Osaka is the place where grand sumo wrestling matches are held.

Rules

All sumo wrestling matches begin and end with the wrestlers bowing to each other. In a tournament, wrestlers fight one match per day. A tournament lasts for 15 days. The lower rank of wrestlers fight a match every two days. Wrestling takes place in a ring called dohyo which is 4.55 m in diameter. It is made of clay and mixed with sand.

The two white lines at the centre mark the position of the sumo wrestlers. Wrestlers take on a wrestling name. Each sumo match is judged by five shimpan (judges). Though the referee declares the winner, the shimpan can deliberate and declare another winner if they do not agree with the decision. Sumo wrestlers fight for ranks. Yokozuna is the highest rank in sumo wrestling.

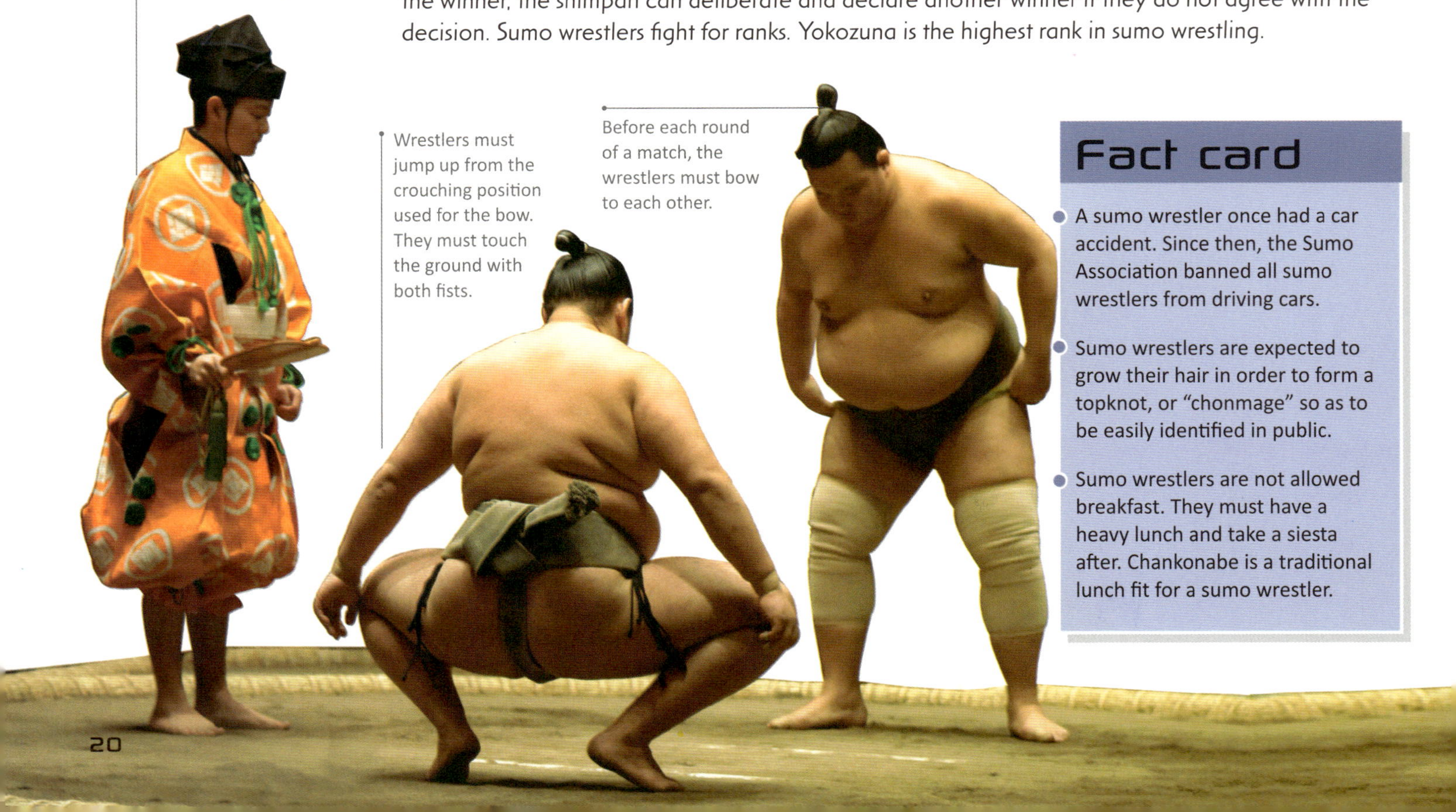

The gyōji is a referee who watches over the match. The onstage gyōji declares the winner while the offstage gyōji declares the winning move.

Wrestlers must jump up from the crouching position used for the bow. They must touch the ground with both fists.

Before each round of a match, the wrestlers must bow to each other.

Fact card

- A sumo wrestler once had a car accident. Since then, the Sumo Association banned all sumo wrestlers from driving cars.
- Sumo wrestlers are expected to grow their hair in order to form a topknot, or "chonmage" so as to be easily identified in public.
- Sumo wrestlers are not allowed breakfast. They must have a heavy lunch and take a siesta after. Chankonabe is a traditional lunch fit for a sumo wrestler.

Taekwondo

Taekwondo is a traditional Korean martial art. It is popular for its athletic and strong kick moves. It is developed from a combination of Korean fighting styles like taekkyeon, gwonbeop and sunbak.

Origin

Taekwondo was developed by a group of Korean martial artists in the period between the 1940s and the 1950s. However, during World War II, the Japanese had occupied Korea and prohibited the practice of any form of self-defence.

In 1992, the World Taekwondo Federation (WTF) was formed for the Olympic Games and taekwondo was included in the 1992 modern Olympic Games.

The name "taekwondo" was given by General Choi Hong Hi who also founded the International Taekwondo Federation (ITF) in 1966. The name translates to "foot, hand, the way" or "the way of the foot and hand". He also co-wrote the Encyclopaedia of Taekwondo.

Players wear helmets to muffle kicks to the head.

This player is attempting a kick to the head. It is one of the most complex taekwondo kicks.

The "hogu" or chest protector is worn to muffle the effect of kicks.

Rules

Taekwondo is played for rank. A typical taekwondo competition involves moves of sparring, breaking, patterns and "hosinsul", which is self-defence. Only sparring moves are allowed in the WTF Olympic competitions. The matches are split into the point sparring and Olympic sparring competitions. In point sparring, all strikes are made with light contact against the opponent. The timer is paused with each strike. In Olympic sparring, the timer keeps ticking as each full contact strike is counted for scoring. The move for "turning behind kick" is given two points, a back kick is given three points while a spinning kick to the head is given four points.

While the chest and head are open to the opponent, players are required to wear helmets and chest protectors to muffle the effect of the kicks.

The colour of the belt is based on the rank of the player. Black belt is the highest rank.

Fact card

- The term "taekwondo" literally means the art of kicking and punching, in Korean.
- In certain formats of the sport, a spinning or jumping kick is worth twice the points of a standing kick.

Judo

The word "judo" means "gentle way". Judo is the form of Japanese modern martial art. The essence of this sport is somewhat similar to the story of David and Goliath in the way that judo's prominent feature is its competitive attitude to throw the opponent on the ground.

To ensure that players remain safe, they need to practice ukemi.

This practitioner is using a mix of throwing and grappling technique.

Participants cannot deviate from their training while performing a move.

Origin

The sport of judo had been developed by a man called "Jigoro Kano". During the westernisation period of Japan, Jigoro became the victim of hostel bullies and he took martial art lessons to defend himself. The sport of judo is based greatly on another form of martial art called "jiu-jitsu". However, Kano wanted this art form to have a wider role in society than simply being a form of self-defence.

Judo emphasises upon free practice, along with using the traditional form of fighting, called "katas". It was in 1899 that the set of rules for judo were crafted.

Judo became an official sport of the Olympic Games since the 1964 Olympics.

The two fighters are practicing the throwing technique. The one that is being thrown needs to know ukemi.

Gameplay

There are three basic techniques in judo called "waza"; nagewaza, which is a throwing technique, katamewaza, which is a grappling technique and atemiwaza, which is a striking technique. The permitted moves from each technique are clearly defined. While practicing, judo practitioners follow ukemi, which is a technique of breaking falling, to reduce the injuries in a game. All judo practitioners must succeed in ukemi before competing.

Judo competitions are done in different weight divisions. The weight divisions are different for men and women. The first category for men begins at under 60 kg and ends at over 100 kg. For women, the first category is under 48 kg and over 78 kg. To ensure that the contests are fair, participants are not allowed to fight someone outside their category.

Fact card

- Sambo and Brazilian jiu-jitsu are derived from judo.

Brazilian Jiu-jitsu

Brazilian jiu-jitsu is derived from judo. It is a combat sport, which focuses on grappling and ground fighting techniques. It is all about technique. If one knows the proper technique, they can fight against anyone outside of their weight class.

Origin

As suggested by the name of the sport, Brazilian jiu-jitsu (BJJ) originated in Brazil, in 1909. Geo Omori started the first school and went on to teach many noteworthy persons, including Luiz Franca.

Another major proponent of the art was Mitsuyo Maeda, who was a student of Jigoro Kano himself. He also trained Carlos Gracie and today the name of the Gracie Family is synonymous with Brazilian jiu-jitsu.

Kodokan judo was unknown to the Brazilians in the early twentieth century. The sport was mistakenly referred to as "jiu-jitsu". Though it was a misonomer, the name still remains to this day.

The grappling on the ground technique gained immense popularity. As a result, joint-locks and submission holds became the prominent features of Brazilian jiu-jitsu.

A major portion of the fight takes place on the ground. Even if an attacker brings the defending practitioner down, the latter can still take lead.

Rules

The core of Brazilian jiu-jitsu is to use a small attack to defeat a big and strong opponent. To nullify the advantage of height and reach, the practitioner attempts to get his/her opponent on the ground.

Once on the ground, a variety of joint-locks and chokeholds are applied on the opponent. Performing joint locks, targeting knee, ankle and spine joints are banned because of high chance of permanent damage, if executed successfully. Chokes should also typically target the carotid artery rather than the windpipe to avoid injury.

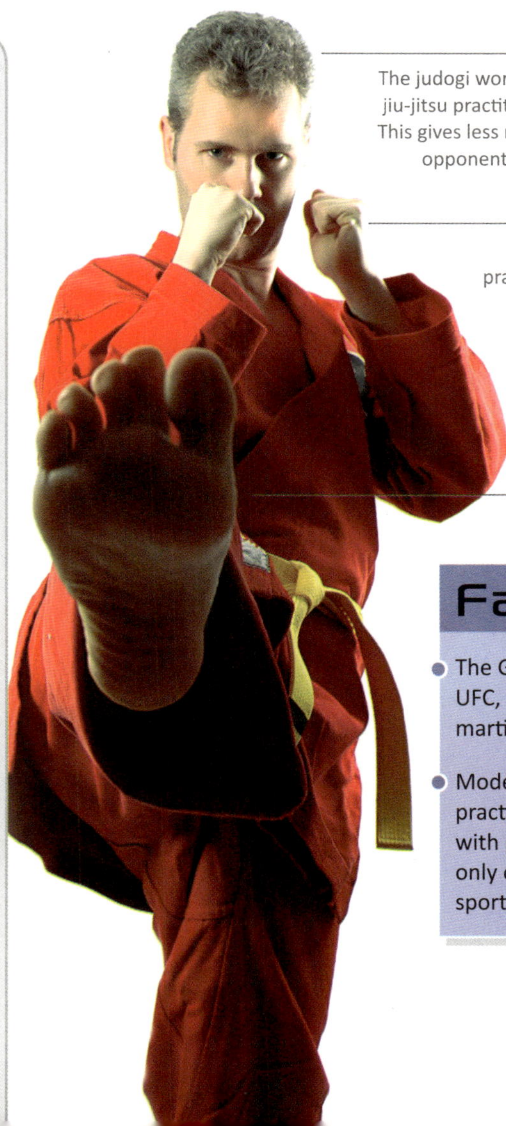

The judogi worn by a Brazilian jiu-jitsu practitioner is tighter. This gives less material for the opponent to manipulate.

The Brazilian jiu-jitsu practitioner also wears a judogi.

The kicking and striking techniques used in judo also apply here. But as a means to bring the player to the ground.

Fact card

- The Gracies went on to found the UFC, and inventing the sport of mixed martial arts.
- Modern Brazilian jiu-jitsu practitioners are looking to do away with points in scoring and focussing only on submission holds to make the sport more spectator friendly.

Boxing

In proverbial usage, phrases like "keeping the fists up" and "staying on the feet" are very famous, which have their origin from "pugilism" or more commonly known as boxing. It is a sport of speed, strength, endurance and reflexes. It uses the pattern of weakening and knocking down the opponent. This is done by delivering sharp punches with the gloved hands.

Origin

Boxing is a part of both Commonwealth and Olympic Sports. The first instance of fist fighting occurred in the kingdom of Sumeria, over 5000 years ago. Boxing is said to have been developed from fist fighting.

The most famous instances of the sport were recorded at the Olympics in ancient Greece. In fact, the term "pugilism" comes from the Greek word "pyx" meaning "with a closed fist". In Rome, the fighters used leather thongs as gloves. Slowly, those were replaced with iron spikes to cause more damage. Fist fighting was outlawed in 393 CE because it was excessively brutal.

All of these changed in 1867, when John Graham Chambers came up with a new set of rules called the "Queensberry Rules". He named it after the ninth Marquess of Queensberry. The rules made boxing both safe and socially acceptable by introducing protection and different weight classes.

Rules

Modern boxing follows the Marquess of Queensbury rules. Each match consists of a number of predetermined rounds, each lasting for three minutes. The maximum number of rounds allowed is 12, which earlier used to be 15. There is a one-minute break in between each of the rounds, during which the players re-strategise and drink water. The boxers retreat to their individual corners during these breaks to receive medical attention for injuries that might have occurred.

A referee is present to ensure that the boxers stick to the rules of the game. Punches are not allowed to the neck, groin area or anywhere below the belt.

Fighting gear

Head guard: Boxers need to wear head guards to protect their heads from serious blows.

Gloves: Gloves reduce the impact of punches against the opponent's body, and also keep the boxer's hand safe.

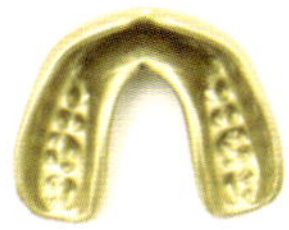

Mouth guard: Boxers can hit each other on the mouth. The mouth guard protects the teeth during punches to the face.

Rope: A boxer touching the ropes during a knockout cannot be attacked.

Neutral corner: After a KO, the standing boxer must immediately stand at the neutral corner and stop fighting.

Referee: A referee presides over the match and gives time out if he sees a boxer misbehaving.

Hit the dock: During an active match, boxers can use the ropes for their strategic moves.

A "knockout" is when a boxer falls on the floor after being hit by the opponent. If the opponent does not get up before a count of 10 by the referee, he is considered to be "knocked out". This is called "KO" and the referee declares the boxer left standing, the winner. But if the opponent gets up before the referee counts up to 10, it is considered a "knockdown". Three knockdowns count as a knockout and a "TKO" wins the match. Boxing is classified into weight divisions from light flyweight to heavyweight or super heavyweight. Fighters usually do not fight outside their weight class. Boxers may not hold each other in "clinches". They cannot hit with knuckles of a bare closed fist.

Wall of fame

The greatest boxer of all time, Muhammad Ali has pioneered the idea of speed being an important element in heavyweight boxing.

Mike Tyson became the youngest boxing champion at the age of 20. He is also remembered for biting off an opponent's ear.

One of the most famous boxers, Floyd Mayweather was undefeated after 49 bouts and reportedly makes USD 100 million per fight.

Fact card

- During a boxing match, Muhammad Ali would "trash-talk" in order to distract his opponents or make them too angry to focus.
- Bare-knuckle boxing was so physically damaging that the disfigured faces and the typically visible cauliflower ears, distinguished the boxers, from the rest. This type of boxing is not allowed in professional competitions.

Kickboxing

Kickboxing is a form of stand-up combat sport, combining the techniques of kicking and punching. Kickboxing has gained immense popularity both as a means of general fitness and as a form of self-defence. It is a full contact combat sport that emphasises upon the use of the legs and arms.

This is a complex kickboxing technique where one foot is on the ground and another raised high and kept straight.

Origin

Kickboxing is a term which refers to many forms of martial arts like Japanese kickboxing (based on karate), muay thai (from Thailand) or savate (from France). As a result, it is difficult to figure out the origin of this game.

The current definition includes any of the varied martial arts, which use hands and feet for striking the opponent. While some of these have developed independently, others are based on existing forms.

The idea of kickboxing gained a lot of popularity in the 1970s both in the USA and Japan. A variety of organisations, like the World Kickboxing Association and the International Kickboxing Federation host bouts with different rules.

Rules

Kickboxing is primarily a full contact striking sport. This means that the fighters are allowed to strike each other, but may not grab, hold or throw their opponent as seen in judo, wrestling or boxing.

There are two contact rules:

1 Contact is allowed but only above the waist in North America.

2 Contact is allowed even below the waist, except for the groin area in the rest of the world.

Practitioners wear boxing gloves to muffle the intensity of the punches on their hands.

The opponent has struck this practitioner below the chin. This is a legal move in kickboxing.

For both the sets, the groin area is off limits. Striking with knees and elbows is prohibited, though certain bouts may allow kicking with the shin. Fighters use protective gear for their hands, shins and head.

Like in boxing, practitioners protect their face. In kickboxing, they protect it from the opponent's kicks and punches.

Fact card

- Jean-Claude Van Damme popularised kickboxing through his 1989 film "Kickboxer".

Muay Thai

Muay Thai is a form of martial art which was developed in Thailand. This combat sport is the modified version of an ancient form of martial arts.

Origin

It is an old tradition in Thailand for soldiers, warriors and fighters to fight unarmed in a combat arena. The various forms of unarmed combat sports were referred to with the umbrella term, "Muay Boran". Muay Thai is a full contact sport, which developed around the 1920s from Muay Boran. The Thai King Rama VII was responsible for formalising the rules of modern Muay Thai, as it is being played today.

He built the first fighting arena and introduced the concept of using protective gear in the fight. Muay Thai gained popularity in the rest of the world when practitioners of this art defeated those of the other martial art forms.

Muay Thai focuses on conditioning the fighter's body. While practicing, fighters strike punching bags and hard surfaces to harden and strengthen their hands, feet, elbows, knees and shin.

These two fighters are involved in a vertical grappling move.

Practitioners wear special shoes to protect the feet.

Muay Thai practitioners wear boxing gloves on their hands for safety reasons.

Muay Thai is usually practised without a shirt or with light cotton tanks.

Fact card

- Muay Thai is the national sport of Thailand.
- Muay Thai's prevailing technique is attrition. Fighters gladly accept blows, so they can deliver one in return. It is all about who lands the hardest blow.

Rules

The World Muay Thai Council has set professional rules for the sport. According to the rules, use of hands, fists, knees, elbows, shin and feet are allowed as the striking surfaces. Fighters may also use vertical grappling techniques, which means that they clinch the opponents, in order to strike them with the knees or shin.

Muay thai fighters wear gloves and hard groin guards as protective gears. Muay Thai fights are preceded by ritual dances and prayers from the competing fighters. However, of late, fighters from different countries have chosen to skip this step.

FILA Grappling

There are some forms of sports that died out in ancient times, only to be revived later. FILA grappling is such a form of sport. However, FILA has ceased sanctioning this sport since 2013.

This is a grappling technique where the kneeling practitioner is in the dominant position. He cannot hold the pose for more than three seconds.

Origin

FILA grappling is a hybrid combat sport, influenced by multiple elements of freestyle wrestling, Greco-Roman wrestling, Brazilian jiu-jitsu and sambo. Grappling focusses on ground combat, as a result of which, the advantage of greater reach is completely nullified. The majority of grapplers are compact and stocky, with a low centre of gravity.

FILA grappling focuses on submission rather than takedowns or pins. Hence, the moves allowed in this sport are of a greater variety than the ones offered in other forms. The chokehold technique is allowed in this sport. Grappling faces a lot of criticism for being barbaric, and has a higher rate of injuries than other full contact sports.

Rather than takedowns, judges are looking for the opponent to submit to defeat.

Fact card

- The first FILA grappling competition was held in 2007.
- FILA dropped both grappling and amateur mixed martial arts after the International Olympic Committee discussed dropping wrestling from the Olympics Games.
- While shoes are optional, both players must wear it if one chooses to.

Gameplay and gear

Grappling has two classes; for the competitors with uniform (gi) and those without (no-gi). But the wrestlers in the "no-gi" category need to follow certain norms in what they wear. They must use only FILA approved shorts and tight fitting rasher vests. They can even choose to forego the vest during practice or training. However, it is a must in professional competitions. Players can choose to fight barefoot. If they choose to wear footwear, it must be approved by FILA. The gi and no-gi uniforms are set in different standards.

Points are awarded for getting into a dominant position and holding it for longer than a few seconds. Unless the wrestler manages to change position after three seconds, no extra points are awarded and holding the dominant position becomes a losing tactic if it is held for a long time.

The main purpose behind the sport is to make the opponent give up the fight. Until one player gives up, the fight will continue. The fighters could come from different backgrounds like wrestling, jiu-jitsu and so on. As long as they follow rules and are aware of the grappling techniques, they are allowed to partake in the competition.

Sambo

Sambo is a Russian sport that is based on various styles of martial arts. It is an acronym for Samozashchita Bez Oruzhiya, which is Russian for "self-defence without weapons".

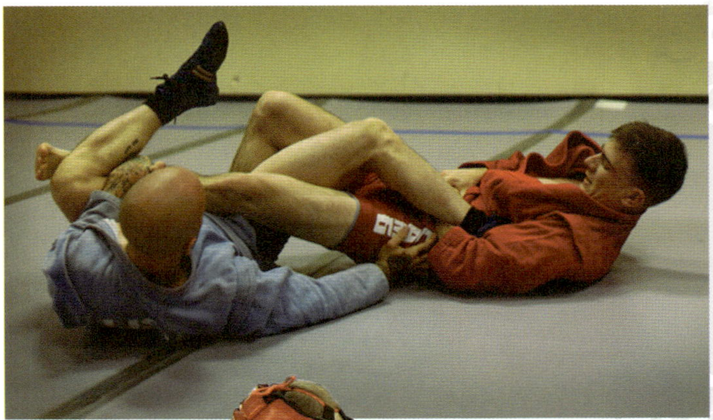

Origin

Sambo originated and evolved in the Soviet Union during the late 1920s and early 1930s. It was taught by the Soviet Army to its soldiers as a form of basic self-defence.

Anatoly Kharlampiev is widely recognised as the father of sambo. Drawing from various styles of judo, jiu-jitsu, karate and native wrestling, Kharlampiev built upon the work of his predecessors, Vasiliy Oshchepkov and Viktor Spiridonov, to build sambo as it is known today.

Gameplay

Sambo is practiced in three distinct styles, each with its own rules. Each requires some sort of uniform and has a ranking system, which ranges from Novice to Uchitel i.e., teacher, with each rank having three sub-stages.

Sambo was first demonstrated in the Olympic Games' Opening Ceremony in 1980. Several books have erroneously reported that it was a demonstration sport at the 1980 Summer Olympics which were held in Moscow in the USSR.

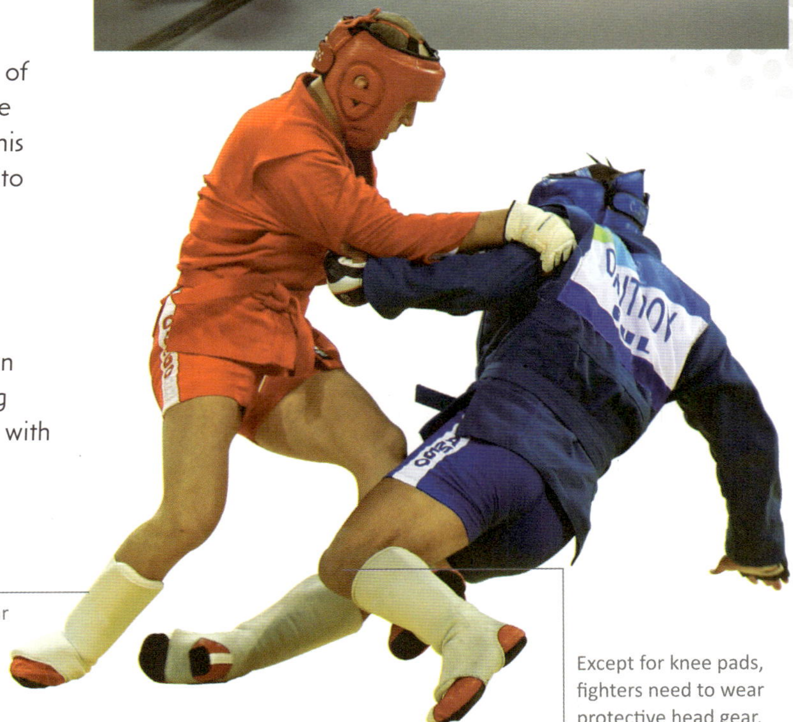

Fighters need to wear special socks that go over the footwear.

Except for knee pads, fighters need to wear protective head gear, gloves and shoes.

Fact card

- Sambo is recognised as the third form of wrestling by FILA but it is not an Olympic sport.
- The sambo community began its own organisation in 1985 called the "Federation International Amateur Sambo" (FIAS), which split into two groups in 1993 with the same name and logo. They were differentiated by being called FIAS East and FIAS West.
- It was recognised as an official sport in 1938 by the USSR All-Union Sports Committee.

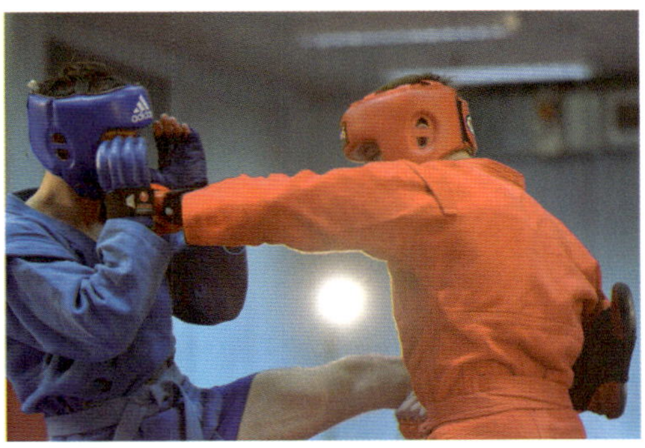

Combat sambo – It was developed more for military applications than for competitive training or sport. It resembles mixed martial arts. This is an "anything goes" sport, where grappling and striking are allowed, and extensive pads and protection need to be used for the safety of the fighters.

Sport sambo – Sport sambo is similar to Olympic judo, with minor differences. Using certain leg-lock techniques are permitted but chokeholds are banned.

Freestyle sambo – Freestyle sambo is a variation of the main style of sambo. It is mainly used in the USA. It does not allow the use of striking, but some chokehold techniques are allowed.

A sambo practitioner wears a red or blue jacket. It is called a "kurtka" or a "sambovka".

A sambo practitioner also wears a belt with shorts. It is the same colour as the top that the practitioner wears.

Mixed Martial Arts

Mixed martial arts or MMA is a form of full-contact combat sport, which includes both striking and grappling techniques. This is one of those sports which were brought back after they died out in the past.

Origin

Mixed martial arts is a fluid sport in which a variety of styles are practiced. It is very similar to the Greek sport of "pankration". Reportedly, no-holds-barred fights have taken place in the ancient times which resembled the mixed martial arts technique. Those were the closest to "real fighting", since very few rules were imposed on the fighters.

However, after the fall of the Greek and Roman civilisations, no-holds-barred fighting on a professional level died down. It was brought back in the late nineteenth century. Then it spread as various cultures across the globe came in contact with each other.

Rules

By design, mixed martial arts has very few rules. The rules that are a part of the sport have been formed to ensure that the fighters do not encounter any permanent physical damage. For example, fish hooking, eye gouging, head butting or stomping on an opponent is not allowed.

Earlier, underground fighting rings were built for the purpose of conducting MMA matches. These sprang up all over Europe, Japan and parts of the Americas. These fights used a combination of various martial arts. Today, MMA fights occur in cages rather than in rings.

MMA fights are conducted in three to five rounds, each of five minutes, with a one-minute break in between. An MMA match is won outright, when an opponent either tapped out or knocked out.

The most recognisable person in the field of mixed martial arts is Bruce Lee. He famously said, "The best fighter is not a boxer, karate or judo man. The best fighter is someone who can adapt to any style, to be formless, to adopt an individual's own style and not follow the system of styles."

MMA is popular for being a sport that defines the muscles of the body and keeps the body lean.

MMA uses various fighting techniques where fighters either use stand-up or horizontal grappling techniques.

Male MMA fighters choose to go shirtless to feel comfortable in the cage.

Like in other combat sports, there is a referee who presides over the match.

Depending on the contest, opponent's can back each other up against the cage wall.

MMA fights occur in octagonal cages rather than in rings.

Sprawl-and-brawl is a stand-up fighting technique.

Clinch fighting is a method of holding the opponent for takedowns.

MMA allows kicks, punches, grappling and clinching techniques.

As the sport has evolved, more rules have been added to make it appealing to a global audience. All contestants must use fingerless gloves during the matches. Matches are divided into different weight classes, from flyweight to super heavyweight.

All MMA players wear fingerless gloves as they punch with their knuckles.

Usually, the thumb is left completely out of the glove as it is not really used in MMA for fighting.

The gloves are soft and padded so the fighters get a reduced impact of the punch.

Wall of fame

Cain Velasquez is a two-time winner of the heavyweight Ultimate Fighting Championship.

Jon Jones is a light heavyweight UFC player. He has been the eight-time defender of the title.

Jose Aldo has been a seven-time defending champion of the UFC, in the featherweight category.

Fact card

- Vale tudo is a Brazilian form of MMA, which literally means "anything goes".
- Royce Gracie initially popularised MMA by throwing open challenges to anyone who wished to fight him. He was successful against much bigger opponents, which added to his popularity.
- Along with MMA, there are other "hybrid" martial art forms that focus on self-defence. Krav Maga is one such sport. MMA is a popular self-defence sport.

Jousting

Previously, it has been talked about how unarmed combat decreased in popularity during the Medieval Ages. Instead, the Knights preferred to fight with weapons on horseback. Jousting is one such Medieval Age sport.

Origin

During the early fourteenth century, the core concept of jousting was rooted in the tactics of heavy cavalry. Fully armoured knights would charge into infantry to break up their formation. The lance was developed for this initial charge to penetrate deeply. The knight would then drop the lance and use a sword, mace or axe.

The sport of jousting followed the same format initially. Two knights would charge and attempt to hit each other with a lance. And after the attempt, they would resort to the use of close-quarter weapons. Slowly, jousting evolved into more of a spectator sport. Knights would now charge at each other and attempt to break lances on the other's armour or shield. They would then go back to the starting point and start again.

These horsemen are from the same team. Jousting is also done in teams for special occasions.

Gameplay

Jousting is carried out on a strip, divided into two halves by a rail. The knights, ready with the lances, charge towards each other. The aim is to break a lance, while not getting hit by the opponent. The jousters wear heavy jousting armours made especially to withstand a hit. The lances used are designed to break rather than penetrate.

This horseman is competing with the rival who has descended from his horse.

Matches are carried on for a number of "lances," i.e., rounds. The knight with the higher number of broken lances wins. Another way to win is to make the opponent climb off the horse. This is an automatic win, regardless of the score otherwise. The player who loses a jousting match, often forfeits his armour and horse to the winner.

In some countries, even the horse is given protective gear to wear on the face and body.

Fact card

- The word "joust" literally means "to meet". Early jousts were conducted in grand fairs.
- The modern sport of tent pegging has evolved from jousting.